The
Perfectly
Behaved
Gentleman

The Perfectly Behaved Gentleman

Robert O'Byrne

Illustration by
Lord Dunsby

CICO BOOKS

LONDON NEW YORK

Published in 2014 by CICO Books
An imprint of Ryland Peters & Small Ltd
20–21 Jockey's Fields   519 Broadway, 5th Floor
London WC1R 4BW   New York, NY 10012

www.rylandpeters.com

10 9 8 7 6 5 4 3 2 1

A CIP catalog record for this book is available
from the Library of Congress and the
British Library.

ISBN: 978 1 78249 161 3

Printed in China

Editor: Rosanna Lewis
Designer: Jerry Goldie
Illustrator: Lord Dunsby
aka Steve Millington

For digital editions, visit
www.cicobooks.com/apps.php

Contents

Introduction

*"Never impose on others
what you would not choose
for yourself."*

Confucius

In 1981, the Anglo-Irish writer Molly
Keane published a much-lauded novel
called Good Behaviour. The title is
intentionally ironic, since the one thing
Keane's main characters never did was to
behave well. That most of them were
consistently unhappy and unfortunate
surely had something to do with a
collective failure ever to engage in good
behavior. Had they shown more kindness,
more consideration, and more
thoughtfulness, their lives would most
likely have been much better.

The same is true for the rest of us. What has become known as the Golden Rule of Reciprocity proposes that we should all behave as we would want other people to behave toward us. This concept has appeared in many different philosophies and religious faiths over the millennia. The teachings of Confucius, for example, include the master being asked by a disciple: "Is there one word that may serve as a rule of practice for all one's life?" The master replied: "Is not reciprocity such a word? Never impose on others what you would not choose for yourself." Similarly, in St. Matthew's Gospel, Christ is quoted as saying "Do unto others as you would have them do unto you."

When you see it in print or hear it said, the underlying merit of the Golden Rule is self-evident. In fact, the advantages of behaving well at all times and in all places are so obvious that they ought not need elucidation. Too often, however, they do. Why might this be the case? Why does each generation need to be reminded how to behave properly?

One explanation for the consistent failure to appreciate this incontrovertible truth lies in the widespread confusion that muddles good behavior with etiquette. The two are quite different. Etiquette is largely ritualistic, its primary function being to allow one member of a particular tribe to identify another and to shut out everyone else. Etiquette is exclusive.

Good behavior, on the other hand, is inherently inclusive. Its function is to demonstrate courtesy and consideration toward other people and to put them at their ease. Just as Confucius, Christ, and many more teachers have proposed, good behavior means treating everyone you encounter the way you want them to treat you.

It's easy to bemoan the absence of good behavior in today's world, but we should not allow ourselves to become too stuffy on the subject. The spirit of the present age inclines toward the casual: we must perforce do the same and accept that we live in informal times, when many of the rules that used to govern social interaction—rules generally based on traditional etiquette—have been set aside.

In theory, the result of this should be that we're now all equally well-behaved. In practice, of course, that's rarely the case. Instead of increasing good behavior, social democracy seems to have encouraged its widespread decline. Don't allow this trend to affect you or your conduct. Recognize that politeness, courtesy, and consideration will always be preferable to their opposites, no matter what the character of the time.

"Manners maketh man."

"Manners maketh man," proposed the fourteenth-century Bishop of Winchester, William of Wykeham. The Middle Ages was a far rougher period than our own (anyone care for ritual disembowelment?), but even then the value of good behavior was understood. Courtesy and consideration should pervade every area of your life, not just those moments when you're in company. Dropping litter, for example, or talking loudly on the phone whilst on public transport, are instances of discourtesy, indicating want of thoughtfulness toward your fellow human beings and the environment we share: remember that next time a piece of gum stuck to the sole of your shoe embeds itself in your carpet at home.

It also helps to keep in mind that what is deemed acceptable in your particular social circle or country might not be judged the same way somewhere else. A perfectly behaved gentleman will be acceptable in any part of the world because he understands the necessity of adapting to differing circumstances and doesn't apply the same rules on all occasions. When traveling, for example, take the trouble to find out what's regarded locally as good and bad practice and temper your behavior accordingly. In some cultures, holding your girlfriend's hand on the street or wearing shorts in a building associated with religious practice is unacceptable. Don't do it unless you want to flout custom and cause gratuitous offence, neither of which are ever actions of the well-behaved.

Regardless of your mood or the moment, always say please and thank you (and learn how to say them in the language of whatever country you're visiting). Don't assume your gratitude will be understood: make it audible.

Apologize if you've done something wrong. Apologize even if you don't think you've done something wrong but another person does. "Sorry" is a small word, but it can make a big difference, and so can its absence.

Be punctual. Only the selfish are habitually late.

Learn to listen. The best talkers are those who hear what's being said to them.

Be cheerful. It'll make you feel better and everyone else you encounter, too. Bad behavior is often inspired by bad temper: avoid one and you're likely to avoid the other.

Practice these simple rules and it is certain that you will be universally known, respected, and admired as a perfectly behaved gentleman.

Chapter 1

Behaving Perfectly at Work

—————◆—————

Unless you're a self-employed hermit, it's likely your professional life will involve interaction with other people. In the work environment make things easy for yourself, and for the advancement of your career, by adopting a manner that's courteous and engaging. You probably won't like some of your colleagues but that doesn't mean you can't get along with them on a nine-to-five basis.

Looking for a Job

Especially at the start of your working life, finding a job—any job—is never easy. However, inadequate preparation and presentation will make the task more difficult: give both the attention they deserve and you stand a far better chance of securing employment.

For example, your C.V. (curriculum vitae) or resumé, the document you forward to prospective employers, should be smart and sharp, with absolutely no spelling mistakes or grammatical errors. Short is better than long; if you want to produce something substantial, write a book. Don't lie, don't exaggerate, don't make claims you can't substantiate: particularly since the advent of the Internet, flexibility with the truth is inadvisable because sooner or later you will be found out. Include details of a couple of people who can testify to your superior abilities, but check first that they are happy to have their names mentioned.

If you're mailing a C.V. and want it returned, enclose a stamped and self-addressed envelope.

Update your C.V. annually. Your career will change and the record of it should do the same. That way, whenever you apply for a new position, the relevant documentation will be ready to go.

When applying for a job, discover everything you can beforehand about the company and the specific vacancy. This is where an Internet search comes in useful. Not only will you be well prepared for an interview, but also you'll have a much better idea about whether this is actually the right position and business for you. Ask around about the organization. What sort of reputation does it have as an employer? Are staff happy? Does it enjoy good industrial relations?

If you are called for an interview, persuade someone you know to run through a mock version (preferably without the mocking) a night or two beforehand. Give whoever's playing the role of interviewer all the information you've gathered so that you can be asked the kind of questions you're likely to face on the day itself. This will help you prepare your responses to those queries that, no matter how often posited, invariably leave most of us stumped, such as "What makes you believe you're suitable for this position?" or "Where do you see yourself in five years' time?"

Be punctual for your interview. The panel you are going to face will most likely be running late, but you can't afford that luxury. Dress well. When researching the company, try to find out about any dress code (official or unofficial) and conform to it on the day of the interview. But take the trouble to be just that little bit smarter than normal. If it's a jeans-style Internet business, for example, on the day of the interview your jeans will be new, from a good label, and have a snug fit.

Be punctual for your interview. The panel you are going to face will most likely be running late, but you can't afford that luxury.

During the interview, your formal qualifications will probably take up the least time, since the panel will have read through your beautifully presented C.V. Treat the occasion as an opportunity to sell yourself. Avoid being cocky or appearing arrogant, but equally steer clear of excessive modesty or self-effacement. Your sound preparation will now prove its worth as you demonstrate that you're efficient, well-informed, and, above all, keener than any of the other candidates. Don't wait to be asked questions; throw in a few and turn the occasion into a conversation. Have a couple of queries prepared and always ask about the specifics of the job you've applied for. A certain amount of nervousness is permissible. After all, you're facing the possibility of rejection, so this is a vulnerable moment.

The day after, send a short letter or email to the company saying thank you for the opportunity to interview for a position there. End by saying how much you look forward to a speedy response to your application.

On the Job

Congratulations, you've got the position. Now confirm to your new employers that they made the correct choice. No matter how low your place in the company hierarchy, always perform to the very best of your abilities. If you choose to do your job in a poor or slovenly fashion, it's highly unlikely you will ever be offered anything better. Employers rightly judge staff by how well they carry out their work on a daily basis; you will be assessed favorably if you prove committed and industrious. Countering that you're not paid enough to do the work any better will always be met with the same response: if you don't like the job, please feel free to leave.

Employers judge staff by how well they carry out their work; you will be assessed favorably if you prove committed and industrious.

Be enthusiastic, but not to the extent of irritating your co-workers. You're less likely to find the job intolerable if you bring a degree of gusto to the enterprise. Avoid complaining about your job—that it's badly paid, that you're given too much to do, that it's repetitive, that you're stuck in a rut—because listening to you is a bore, and that sort of talk doesn't change your circumstances. To reiterate: if the job doesn't work, it's time to move on.

If you've been given a uniform, keep it clean and tidy. Don't allow dirt or stains to accumulate; have the clothes washed or dry-cleaned regularly. That way you'll look better and feel better, too. You won't make a good impression on your bosses and the general public if you turn up for work looking slovenly. While many jobs don't require employees to wear a formal uniform, there is likely to be an unofficial dress code. Regardless of your personal preferences, you must comply with it. The larger the company, the more conformity of dress is expected among staff. Keep your more outré clothes for time outside the workplace: the corporate environment rarely welcomes mavericks (that's why they tend to start their own businesses). Stand out from your fellow workers through the quality of your work, not because of your nose piercings or colorful hair.

Tidy your desk or workstation. The job will be accomplished better and faster if you can find what you want when you want it. Learn the art of discarding whatever's no longer necessary. If you haven't looked at a file or used a particular item for a couple of months, either store it in a communal space or throw it away. Despite

A note on eating at your desk: don't.

the advent of computers, we all still accumulate far too much paper, most of it duplicating material that's easily accessible elsewhere. If there's an additional copy of a document in the building, either in a cupboard or stored electronically, dispose of yours.

A note on eating at your desk: don't. Days later, you'll find a piece of decaying vegetable matter (or worse) wedged in the pages of a file you were reading at the time. Or IT will have to be called because you spilled mayonnaise on your keyboard. Then there's the matter of hygiene: food in the work environment risks leaving behind germs and lingering odors. Why should co-workers have to smell your chicken curry? It is recommended that we all take a couple of breaks from our workstation during the course of the day. Use one of these to eat your lunch elsewhere. You'll come back refreshed after a short break from your (crumb-free) desk.

Your Co-workers

In the work environment you don't necessarily have a choice about whom you're going to meet and spend time with. Even if you're self-employed, you'll sometimes need to interact with other people. Accept this state of affairs and plan to make the experience as pleasant as possible, for them and for you.

Although it's not always easy, do your best to remain on good terms with your colleagues, or at least to give the impression of doing so. No doubt they have personal habits and idiosyncrasies that infuriate you (just as they are maddened by the way you're constantly clearing your throat or "borrowing" their pens), but you must suffer in silence. This is an opportunity to improve your people skills. Life in the workplace differs little from that outside it: in both cases you'll have a better and easier time if you show consideration for other people and their feelings.

In your professional life, there should be no "little people." You want to move upward because that way you get more money, better perks, and possibly a desk with a view out the window. On your climb up the professional ladder, remember to look back as well as forward. Be just as nice to the people below you as to those above. None of us can ever be sure what changes in fortune will occur. The quiet girl who regularly made you tea might suddenly become your boss (or start sleeping with him). Did you forget to thank her every time she handed you a cup? Did you take her for granted? The likelihood is that she'll now do the same thing to you.

Avoid being sucked into office politics. The larger the organization, the more likely it is that some members of staff will get little work done because their days are filled with covert meetings and email exchanges in which the latest twists and turns of an internal power struggle are discussed. As a rule, these people are interested only in the politics of the place, not its betterment. Usually their own careers have stalled and they're never going to get further up the corporate ladder or leave the company. You can do without this distraction.

Similarly, you'll notice how certain co-workers can't resist the allure of the watercooler. In fact, they seem to spend more time fending off dehydration than they do at their desks. Between sips from a paper cup, they will be analyzing everyone else at work. Office gossip is insidious and invidious, and you don't want to be part of it. Start talking about your colleagues and before long they'll start talking about you.

> *Office gossip is insidious and invidious, and you don't want to be part of it.*

Be careful about chatting online within an office. The amusing message you send to one colleague will be forwarded to another twenty—including the subject of your mirth (who's much less entertained than the rest of the office and lodges a complaint with the HR department).

Be a contributor. Don't just do your own work and leave it at that. Offer something extra and most likely you'll receive something extra in return, even if it's only a greater sense of personal satisfaction from a job well done.

Don't be too proud to ask for help, especially if the alternative means you're liable to make a mistake. Ask if you're not sure how to address a superior, use the new piece of hardware, or find your way to the canteen.

Respect other people's space. Before you begin chatting to a colleague, check if this is a convenient moment. Don't hover by anyone talking on the phone. It might be a private call, but even if it isn't, your presence is invasive. Write a quick note or send an

internal message asking the person to get in touch when they're free. Desk perching is inexcusable.

In an open-plan office, keep your voice down, your aftershave light, and your opinions to yourself.

At meetings, make your presence felt but don't dominate. Contribute to the discussion without controlling it. Encourage others to speak before you. This gives you time to prepare your input while becoming aware of their ideas and proposals and analyzing the merits/drawbacks of these. Make your points clearly, attributing at least some of the advantages to people who spoke earlier ("As Jim pointed out just now …"). This has the effect of drawing them onto your side. Seek to achieve consensus as much as is possible. Prepare for compromise: concede on lesser details and you're much more likely to win your principal argument; fight to get your own way on every minor point and you could lose them all. If you are successful, never seek to have the fact that you got what you wanted publicly acknowledged: your victory was probably someone else's defeat. If you draw attention to yourself in this way you risk making enemies unnecessarily.

Prepare for compromise: concede on lesser details and you're much more likely to win your principal argument.

Never meet rudeness with rudeness. It only shows that you're no better than the person who was offensive in the first place, and it can often cause the hostility to escalate. Respond to bad behavior with the observation, "That's very rude." It's not particularly clever, but almost without fail proves effective in silencing the guilty party.

Should the rudeness be habitual and risk interfering with your work, don't try to deal with the matter by yourself. Make a formal complaint, either to your superior or, if your company has one, to the HR department. Be specific rather than general. Present a log of timed and dated incidents of rudeness to back up your complaint and demonstrate how they have adversely affected your performance at work. Many companies have a poor record when it comes to dealing with office bullying and internal strife. The more clearly you show that acting on your complaint will be beneficial for the business, the sooner, and better, it will be dealt with.

Socialize with co-workers in moderation. How you behave with them outside the work environment will affect how they perceive you inside it. Give no hostages to fortune: if you go out for one drink with some colleagues, it turns into several, and by the end of the night you're slurring out your real opinion of the boss or how you lust after Christine in Telemarketing. The next day that information will be traveling around the office and attitudes toward you will be adjusted accordingly. Be discreet and remain cautious about speaking your mind on work-related topics to anyone in the same organization.

Because we spend so much time at work, we are all inclined to develop a variation of Stockholm Syndrome whereby we start to hold colleagues in higher esteem than would be the case if we met them in another

context. Obviously there are occasions, like the Christmas party, when you have to socialize with your co-workers, but don't make a habit of it or you'll become unable to put the intensity of office politics into perspective. There is a big world beyond, and you really ought to have a life outside work.

It's never a good idea, yet it continues to happen: the office romance. No matter how discreet you both believe your behavior to be, fellow workers will find out, and you will thereby provide a fresh topic of conversation for watercooler regulars. It is especially unwise if either or both of you are married or otherwise committed, or if there's a disparity in rank. And if the relationship doesn't last, you'll have the problem of sharing a workplace with your former lover—particularly not fun if the breakup is in any way acrimonious. This could affect your job, your performance, possibly even your prospects in the company.

You and Your Boss

Enjoy a good working relationship with your superiors, but don't try to be their best friend (you have some of those outside work, remember). You want the boss to appreciate your work, which doesn't mean he or she necessarily has to like you: understand the difference. If you're good at your job and work hard, your merits will be noticed.

Whenever possible, turn down invitations to socialize with your boss while making it clear you're grateful for the offer. There are times, however, when saying no might damage your career, while saying yes could advance it. On these occasions, of course, the latter's your only option, so make play outside the office still work to your advantage. Be yourself. Present your boss with much the same person they already know from the office. Avoid drinking too much or being too obsequious. Don't defer excessively, and don't be afraid to assert opinions as you would on any other social occasion.

Stifle the urge to contradict your boss or a senior colleague when the incorrect information is given, the wrong policy decision taken, or bad advice proffered.

A good working relationship with the boss will be hard if the two of you find yourselves in conflict. Since you're an employee, you are more likely to suffer the consequences. Sort out bad blood fast. This could mean you have to eat a certain amount of humble pie, but better a slice now than the entire dish later. In a dispute between boss and underling, the latter has to lose otherwise the former's authority is called into question. Which matters more to you: being right or being employed?

Stifle the urge to contradict your boss or a senior colleague when the incorrect information is given, the wrong policy decision taken, or bad advice proffered. You have your opinions, but harmony in the workplace advises that you keep them to yourself. Or move elsewhere.

If disputes and differences of opinion are a regular occurrence, the problem is not one of principle but of temperament, either yours or your employer's, or both. Maybe you're unsuited to working in a hierarchical environment? Not everyone is a team player or prepared to take direction. You can't change your character, but you can change your circumstances. Look into the possibility of working for yourself, where there'll be only one person to whom you're answerable: you.

Looking for a raise or a better position within the company? Ask and you shall receive, provided your request is made in the right way and at the right time. As in any circumstance where you can't be certain of the outcome, sound preparation is critical. Plan what you want to say and think of good reasons to support your case, with examples of what you've done in the past and intend to do in the future. Don't be despondent if your request is turned down; it may simply be that the company can't afford to offer anyone salary raises right now or the position you seek isn't actually vacant. Ambition and drive will never be frowned upon.

Office Life

Answer a ringing phone. So you're managing director of a company listed on the Stock Exchange with thousands of employees: have you lost the power of speech? No matter how high or low your professional status, you should want the organization with which you're associated to create a good impression. An obvious way to ensure this is by answering every

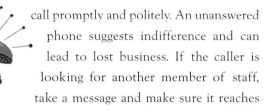

call promptly and politely. An unanswered phone suggests indifference and can lead to lost business. If the caller is looking for another member of staff, take a message and make sure it reaches the intended destination.

Return all calls, reply to all emails, answer all letters. Do so promptly. Take a vow never to leave your place of work without responding to every message you received during the day. Never use the excuse that you've been too busy: do you imagine busy-ness is exclusive to you? Everyone's busy and everyone's getting busier. Some people, however, are organized, and a few of them are also considerate. Make sure you belong to the last category—it will be to your professional advantage. After all, who would you rather do business with: the person who replies to your email promptly or the person who doesn't bother?

Never use the excuse that you've been too busy: do you imagine busy-ness is exclusive to you?

Make phone calls yourself. It's the height of arrogance to have a secretary or assistant call a third party and enquire "Will you hold for …?" The correct response to this question is "No," followed by the sound of a phone line going dead. Who has called whom?

During a telephone conversation, try not to put the other person on hold unless it's absolutely necessary, and then do so for the shortest possible time. If the incoming call is urgent and looks like taking a while, return to the original one, make your apologies, and offer to call back very soon. Remember to do so.

Unless you are participating in a conference call, the speakerphone is unacceptable: pick up the receiver, use the mouthpiece. If it is a conference call, introduce everyone else in the room to the outside caller and make sure each of them says a few words to identify his or her voice.

If you're going to be away from work for some time, advise the receptionist, leave a message to that effect on your voicemail, and inform your colleagues. That way, callers won't be left wondering why they haven't heard back from you for the past fortnight and concluding that you have no manners.

When you call someone at work and have to leave a message, do so clearly and concisely. Give your name and say when you called and why: no mysteries, please. People who don't provide an adequate explanation for their call are more likely to find that it's not returned.

Ideally switch off your personal cellphone when in the office. A less satisfactory alternative is to put it on silent (especially if your ringtone is of the irritating novelty sort) and answer it quickly. Never leave it at work when you've gone out. After it has rung for the third time, your colleagues are entitled to throw the thing out the nearest window.

The office computer is intended for work only. Downloading porn from the Internet is inadvisable: there's a strong possibility that you'll be found out (many companies have installed software to detect the presence of such material). As a result, quite legitimately, you'll be heavily penalized or even fired. Lesser offences, such as using your computer and your work time to write personal emails or an 80,000-word novel, are also liable to come to the notice of your superiors. They'll earn you a reprimand, at the very least. Save all non-work-related activities for your computer at home.

Email is so instantaneous that it encourages reckless spontaneity. Be careful: what you consider spontaneous, somebody else might consider sloppy and unprofessional (with the threat of a correspondingly negative impact on your business). When emailing anything in a professional capacity, rein in your desire to improvise. Prepare a draft, think about who else will see it, and don't overlook the basics of punctuation and grammar, both of which can be corrected speedily on your computer or smartphone.

Moving On

Feeling bored? Think you're under-appreciated? Blocked in your attempt to climb higher? Review your current situation and list the advantages and drawbacks of your present employment. If the latter outweigh the former, it's time to look for another job. You might resist doing so out of fear of the unknown (particularly if you've worked in the same place for many years) and concern that no one else will offer alternative employment, with the inevitable loss of income. All these anxieties are valid, but none of them should stop you leaving your present job, especially if you're working for it but it's not working for you.

Treat fear as a spur, not a hindrance. Draw up two lists, one of your financial outgoings and assets, the other of your qualifications and aspirations. Then make a plan for the year ahead with specific and achievable goals. Yes, in the short term your income will most likely dip, but most of us can find ways of cutting back our expenditure, such as taking fewer vacations or temporarily getting rid of the car. Ask around and you'll discover that people who change jobs rarely say they regret leaving their old position. More often, they say their only regret was not leaving sooner. Hanging onto a job for the sake of your pension is never going to make you happy.

Don't leave a job in anger. You want to depart on good terms with your former employers, not least for the sake of a good reference. And you want to leave with their good wishes, their blessing—and their regret.

Chapter 2

Behaving Perfectly in Public

Whether you're on a plane or in the gym, walking in the park or going to the cinema, you're going to meet other people. In all circumstances, this means showing a certain amount of consideration and an awareness of the difference between private and public space. Above all, remember you're not at home, so don't behave as though you were.

Airplanes, Trains, and Public Transport

Unless you own a private jet, you're liable to find yourself traveling in the company of people you don't know. The fact that formal introductions haven't been performed doesn't mean you should display no interest in anyone else's welfare. On the contrary, this is one more instance when you should treat others as you would wish to be treated: with respect and consideration.

A story doing the rounds tells of a man who found himself unable to read his book on the train journey home one evening because a girl sitting opposite was playing loud music. When he asked her to turn down the volume she ignored him, so he retaliated by reading his book out loud. The girl moved seat.

Ideally there should be no need for you to resort to such tactics, but nor should you be the cause of someone else engaging in this behavior. Whether you're playing a personal music device, speaking on a cellphone, or just having a conversation with the person beside you, keep the volume down: don't assume the rest of us share your outré taste in ghetto lyrics or want to hear details of what you and your pals got up to last night.

Likewise, keep yourself to yourself. Some passengers on public transport behave as though it were their own private bus or train. Remember that the rest of those on board likewise paid to be there. Keep your possessions to yourself and leave vacant seats empty so they can be occupied by other people. Beware of sprawling, either with your limbs or your luggage, lest one of them trips up someone who's passing in the aisle. Share armrests—they weren't installed for your exclusive use.

Never assume the rest of us share your outré taste in ghetto lyrics or want to hear details of what you and your pals got up to last night.

Should you give up your seat on public transport? It used to be that gentlemen would stand for a woman, but, realistically, if she's younger and fitter than you this is absurd: being a woman is not a medical condition. On the other hand, if you do see someone older or frailer than yourself, then do the decent thing and offer your place.

The advent of low-cost airlines and increased security checks has caused travel by airplane to lose whatever residue of glamour it once possessed. "Hell," wrote the philosopher Jean-Paul Sartre, "is other people," and he didn't even live to experience snaking lines for the inspection of hand baggage. Comfort yourself with the thought that while this existential hell is only

temporary for you, it's a way of life for the people who work in airports. Show them consideration, not least because that way they're more likely to respond in kind. Recognize that they are doing their job and that they have heard every excuse—and every sort of abuse—many times before and that it won't make any difference. You are more likely to get what you want, whether it's an upgrade or a speedy passage through customs, by being pleasant than by displaying aggression or resentment. Show empathy: try smiling, engaging in conversation, or using the official's name (if it's visible on a badge).

> *You are more likely to get what you want by being pleasant than by displaying aggression or resentment.*

Some of us travel light, some of us travel as though fleeing political oppression. Understand that if you bring more than the permitted luggage, you will be charged extra. Skip arguments with check-in staff over the size and weight of your bags: this is one battle you cannot win. Plus, you will alienate other passengers waiting to drop off their bags while you engage in a pointless bout of bickering.

Note the gate and time of departure as displayed on your boarding pass. There is no excuse for delaying a flight, particularly if it's because you were lingering in duty-free or didn't hear your name called because you were following a game on the television in the bar.

Once on board, listen to the crew's requests that you step in from the aisle and not block the progress of other passengers. When placing items in an overhead bin, look out for what's already there: someone was planning to wear that once-carefully draped jacket that you reduced to a crumpled heap by stuffing your own possessions on top of it.

Recline with care: take into account the person sitting behind you whose cup of hot coffee will be flung to the ground as you push your seat back. Look behind you, and give notice of your intentions. It's a small thing, but it makes a big difference.

Train yourself to sleep upright. Spare yourself the shame of waking to find your head resting on the shoulder of whoever's in the next seat. Buy an inflatable neck cushion (but please don't wear it while walking around the airport, unless you relish looking ridiculous).

When you land, resist the temptation to be one of those fevered individuals who immediately undo their seatbelts, leap up, and begin snatching their possessions even before the doors have opened. On the other hand, do help other people retrieve their luggage from the overhead bins.

Traveling by Car

Although you're alone inside your own vehicle, don't assume that you can ignore the rest of the world: roads are communal spaces.

Understand that other drivers are not mind readers: if you're planning to make a turn, use your turn signal (indicator). The driver of the car behind will appreciate this, too.

When halted at traffic lights, don't regard the momentary lull as an opportunity to make a phone call or read the newspaper. Lights change with surprising speed, and it is a courtesy to other cars that you are ready to move when they do so.

When turning at a junction or intersection, hook around the car turning in the opposite direction: you learned this rule before taking your driving test, now apply it.

Never stop in a box junction or in the middle of an intersection. Without fail you will still be there when crossing traffic is allowed to move—but can't do so because you're blocking their route.

Pay attention to speed limits. Don't exceed them, but don't drive far below them either, especially if there is traffic behind you. You may be out for a leisurely afternoon spin, but the line of drivers waiting to overtake might be anxious to reach their destination before nightfall: pull over as soon as you can and allow them to pass before continuing on your way. If you encounter a slow driver, don't flash your lights, sound your horn, or tailgate them. Engaging in any or all of these is likely to make the person ahead move at an even slower pace, either through nerves or in revenge for your rudeness. Perceive this as an opportunity to practice your anger-management skills.

Always get out of the way of any small car with obvious and garish modifications. It will be driven at terrifying speed by a boy so young that he's barely able to see over the steering wheel and has yet to begin shaving.

You may be out for a leisurely afternoon spin, but the line of drivers waiting to overtake might be anxious to reach their destination before nightfall.

Likewise, get out of the way of all drivers playing music loudly with all the windows down: their taste will be execrable. You, an impeccably behaved driver, will of course always keep music at a moderate level, particularly when any windows are open.

In the Park and Other Communal Spaces

Watch where you're going. This needs to be said because many people now wear earphones when in transit and as a consequence seem to exist in a personal vacuum. Remember the old rules of the road and look left and right before you step off the sidewalk (pavement), otherwise you and/or someone driving a car or riding a bicycle could have a nasty accident. (For the same reason, drivers and passengers in a car should look to see if there is anyone in the immediate vicinity before opening a vehicle door.)

Understand that the sidewalk is a shared space, not exclusively yours. If walking with a group of friends, allow other pedestrians to pass without having to step into the road and risk injury. Likewise, if you're waiting for a bus or taxi, form an orderly line.

In parks or on a public beach, once more spare a thought for those with whom you're sharing the space. If you want to play soccer with your buddies or hold a frisbee tournament, do so well away from others. Curb the temptation to show off your athletic prowess, no matter how attractive those girls sitting on the grass nearby. Some people like to commune with the stillness of nature; let them do so. Playing music in public, and thereby inflicting your taste on the wider community, is inexcusably selfish.

If you bring your dog to the park or beach, or even just take it for a walk on the local streets, bring a leash. Bear in mind that while you know Fido has a placid disposition, to the rest of the world he's still a very large Rottweiler, and strangers may not appreciate his efforts to be friendly. For obvious reasons of public hygiene, carry a few plastic bags for pooper-scooping. You and your dog don't need to assume responsibility for fertilizing the grass in the local park. Use the plastic bag on every necessary occasion—and not just when you think someone is looking.

Shopping

When passing through a door, look behind you and hold it open if someone is following. Traditionally, it was deemed good manners to hold open doors for the elderly, the infirm, and women, but the last of these will rightly take you to task if you behave as though, being helpless females, they can't manage that big door all by themselves. Today it's probably better to hold a door for anyone passing through it at about the same time as yourself. If someone holds a door for you, say thank you. It's astonishing how often members of the public fail to utter these two small but significant words.

Always shop with a list written in advance. This will prevent you from wandering aimlessly around the mall or supermarket for hours. Unless, of course, that's precisely what you planned to do, in which case you're a bored teen and it's Saturday afternoon.

If you are buying items that must be weighed and/or priced by you before they are taken to the cashier, please remember to do so. Have your cash or card ready when paying for goods; once more, this will speed up the transaction. No matter how rude or uninterested they might be, always show courtesy to shop staff. As in so many other fields of dealing with the public, their work is often repetitive, not least because customers all seem to complain about the same things.

If you feel you've received shoddy service, don't have an arguement on the spot, as you are unlikely to get satisfaction. Ask the person responsible for his or her name and also the name of their superior. Write these down, advise them that you intend to send a formal complaint to the company, and then send a letter or email detailing your problem.

Don't use your cellphone when dealing with staff: how would you like it if the roles were reversed? On the other hand, appreciate that sales staff will always be more interested in talking to each other than to you. After all, you've never met Susan from Soft Furnishings and so can't appreciate the nuances of what she said after work last night.

Cinemas, Theaters, Concert Halls

Talking is allowed at rock and pop concerts, although electronic amplification will probably render anything you say impossible to hear. In other venues, you should refrain from chatting as it will interfere with other patrons' enjoyment of the occasion. One might think this advice unnecessary, but it is  astonishing how often people embark on a conversation in the middle of a play, movie, or symphony concert.

Most venues now make an announcement before performances, requesting that all cellphones and similar devices be switched off. Please obey it. And don't think the actors on stage can't see you reading your texts: your phone's screen lights up and is easily spotted in a darkened auditorium.

The other source of noisy distraction involves the consumption of food. At the theater, symphony, or opera, anything more substantial than hard candy (boiled sweets) is discouraged (although in every such venue there will be a small group of pensioners rustling through a box of chocolates and trying to avoid anything with a chewy center). Similarly, drinks are generally not permitted inside an auditorium on these occasions; if you're really desperate, bring a hip flask.

By contrast, movie-theater owners encourage the consumption of as much food and drink on the premises as possible, presumably to bump up their profits. Many members of the audience respond as though this is their last meal on earth, ladling up enormous containers of full-fat snacks and sugar-laden drinks. You are not obliged to succumb to this frenzy of fast-food ingestion. But if you do yield to temptation, try to make your snacking as quiet as possible: it can be hard to hear dialogue over the soundtrack of a thousand chomping jaws. And please, at the end of the movie, take your trash with you.

The Gym

Especially in mixed venues, wear sufficient clothing and make sure it holds any independent-minded parts of your anatomy firmly in place. On the running machine, for example, only your legs ought to be in motion. There's a wide range of support sportswear that can make sure this is the case.

Especially in mixed venues, wear sufficient clothing and make sure it holds any independent-minded parts of your anatomy firmly in place.

Launder your clothes after every gym visit. They can be old, as long as they're clean. The only exception is your footwear. After a few months, depending on how often you exercise, sneakers (trainers) are liable to start smelling. Invest regularly in a new pair.

For the sake of your fellow gym users, shower before as well as after you exercise, particularly if you've arrived straight from a day's work. You might not notice your own body odor, but other people will.

Don't hog machines. It's an infallible rule that there are never enough to meet demand. Use a piece of equipment only for a set amount of time, clean up fast, and move on. Never be identified as the man who, having finished his workout, remains draped over the machine breathing heavily. (And no heavy grunting, either.) Nor should you engage in showing off. Focus on getting through your program, not on letting everyone else know how incredibly fit you are. If you look at yourself in the mirror, it should be to check that you're doing the exercise correctly, not to admire your toned pecs.

Severe physical exercise of the kind performed at a gym causes us all to sweat. While there's nothing you can do about this, you can ensure that no evidence is left behind. Once you've finished with a piece of equipment, wipe it down. Bring a small, clean towel with you for this purpose. Leave the equipment as you'd wish to find it: put weights and other items back where they're stored and clear any programs you set on a machine.

Chapter 3

Perfect Behavior in Pubs, Clubs, and Restaurants

When you're meeting someone in a public place, get there on time. At least in a private house your host can find something else to do, like grumble about your tardiness. But there are few better ways of making sure a meeting gets off to a bad start than keeping the other party waiting: none of us likes being left for half an hour to nurse a solitary drink or study a menu.

Always, always text or call if you're running behind schedule, otherwise the person biding their time will wonder if one or the other of you has got the date or place wrong. If you are the person waiting, and you've not received any message from the late arrival, feel free to stay only for a certain length of time, perhaps fifteen minutes, and then leave. Anybody who hasn't the manners and consideration to advise you of delay deserves the same in return.

If you're the late arrival, apologize profusely and sincerely when you finally reach your destination. Provide a brief explanation for your delay—there's no need to waste another quarter hour on the state of local roads. And, in turn, a genuine apology should be accepted with good grace.

Pubs and Clubs

Holding seats is permissible only if there are still plenty for other customers. Should the venue be crowded, it's really not a good idea for you to insist on reserving the last remaining chairs for friends who are nowhere to be seen and who might not arrive for another half hour, if at all. Unless you reserved your place, accept that other people have as much right to it as you do.

Particularly in a bar it's incredibly easy to gain a reputation for tightfistedness and, once acquired, it's very hard to shake off.

Pay your way, by either buying your own drinks or, much better, buying a round (or two) for everyone in the group.

Particularly in a bar it's incredibly easy to gain a reputation for tightfistedness and, once acquired, it's very hard to shake off.

When ordering at the bar, wait your turn. If the bartender offers to help you before the person who's been desperately trying to gain his attention for the past ten minutes, have the good grace to point this out. Catching the eye of staff is a skill granted to some people—usually the taller among us—and not others.

If you offer to buy a stranger a drink, accept the possibility that you'll be turned down. If so, accept the refusal with good grace: no really does mean no, it doesn't mean you should repeat the offer. If you don't like rejection, don't put yourself in a situation where it is a possibility. On the other hand, if your offer is accepted, buy whatever the other person requests. You were thinking a mineral water, she asks for champagne: that's the luck of the draw. Again, if you're not prepared to take the risk, avoid the scenario.

Not everyone consumes alcohol in the same quantity, so never force it on other people. There will be a reason your friend is sticking to just a half-pint, anything from having an important interview the following morning to being low on cash and not in a position to buy something for you. Or maybe he just doesn't wish to have a hangover tomorrow morning. Whatever the explanation, or none, allow it.

If you've overdone it (as many of us have in our time), try to be a tidy drunk. That means acknowledging that you've overindulged: there are few more pathetic spectacles than a man roaring "I'm not drunk" before slithering to the ground. Alcohol can encourage pugnacity. Unless you want to spend the night in a police cell and see your name in tomorrow's newspaper reports, suppress the urge to take on the world. Allow yourself to be helped out of the premises and into a cab. Go home and sleep it off, and the following morning call to thank those helpful friends who looked after you.

Never, ever argue with staff in bars and clubs: you may have right on your side but they have might and that's more important. Whether you're being refused admission, informed that you're

Never, ever argue with staff in bars and clubs: you may have right on your side but they have might and that's more important.

not on the guest list, asked to wait your turn, or told to leave, do as requested. Save the heroics for another occasion.

When you're inspired to dance (spurred perhaps by that alcohol consumption), remember the dance floor's not yours alone; you're obliged to share it with other people, so less of the chicken-flapping imitations, please. Sooner or later one of your arms is going to collide with somebody. The same goes for karaoke and similar public performances. Not everyone will relish hearing Harry Nilsson's "Without You" rendered with quite so much expression.

Restaurants

If you're acting as host in a restaurant, arrive before any of your guests. Should you be delayed, call the restaurant and ask the maître d' to apologize on your behalf to anyone who turns up before you. You could also ask that a waiter offer drinks.

If you're a guest of someone else in a restaurant and you get there first, ask for nothing stronger than a glass of iced water. No matter how irritated you feel at being left to thumb the menu, it's not a good idea to run up a hefty drinks tab.

The person playing host ought to decide who sits where, preferably in advance. When there's no designated host or guests, the situation is more fluid. Traditionally, women occupied the inside seats in restaurants and men those on the outside, but what if you're an all-male group? In most circumstances today, we should sit wherever we like. But be conscious of needs and preferences, and don't grab what you think is the best seat. Wait until other people have made their choice and then take whatever's left.

When it comes to ordering, the host (if there is one) makes the main decisions, such as choosing the wine. But of course an attentive host will consult his guests on their preferences and take these into account.

As a guest, the food you order ought to be neither extravagant (so no to the caviar and lobster) nor frugal: you don't want to intimate that you think your host can't afford anything more than the most humble meal. If there's no host, choose whatever you fancy, but prepare for the possibility of disagreement when the check arrives. Ideally, reach consensus over how many courses everyone is having before the waiter comes to take your order. Don't vacillate over a menu long after the rest of the party have made their choices, and don't change your mind, and your order, after you've given the latter to the staff.

Similarly, skip the regrets about what you've got when you see how much better somebody else's food looks or tastes. And don't reach over to help yourself to what's on another plate. You made your choice, so live with the consequences. Besides, it's only one meal, not your last supper.

Food and wine bores, stay away. Please don't become one of those men who think talking about what you're eating and drinking qualifies as conversation, because it doesn't. In particular, understand that when you begin talking about wine, what you're actually doing is displaying your

superior knowledge on the subject, which is hardly going to ingratiate you with other diners.

And put away the camera. The chef isn't Picasso and the food on your plate isn't a work of art. The best way you can show your appreciation is by eating every last morsel, not by tweeting photographs of your food around the planet.

Regardless of the establishment's prestige, fashionability, or number of Michelin stars, not every meal in a restaurant will be equally successful. It is possible that on this occasion the kitchen is having a bad night, or you've been placed next to a riotous office party, or there's a shortage of staff and your group is neglected, or your wine's corked.

Recognize that this can happen in the best places, so although you (or your host) is paying for what has proven to be a less than happy experience, put it into perspective: nobody died (not even of food poisoning, it is to be hoped). If you are a guest, it's not your place to complain. If you are a host, then you may do so, but preferably not in front of your guests: have a quiet word with the manager, seek contact details such as an email address, and give notice that you will be in touch in the coming days. If you're a group of friends and nobody in the party is taking the role of host or guest, designate one of your number as spokesman to discuss the matter with management: you don't all need to get involved. And no rushing to websites to air your grievances. In fact, no rushing to websites having anything to do with food whatsoever: those places are populated by the self-important who believe their opinion on the correct consistency of béchamel sauce deserves to be aired.

Cellphones should always be switched off in a restaurant or

left unanswered. If you're awaiting an urgent call, give the restaurant's phone number and the time you expect to be there.

Stay at your table, rather than flitting from one to another. Moving around the premises demonstrates how terribly popular you are and how the rest of your group doesn't share this good fortune. Once you sit down, remain in your place until it's time to leave. And no waving across the room, either.

Every time you go outside to have a cigarette, you disrupt the rhythm of your table's conversation. No matter how great the nicotine craving, leave the table as seldom as possible.

Be polite to staff. Everyone ought to spend a few days annually working as a waiter: the outcome would be an immediate improvement in behavior among restaurant clientele (and a corresponding increase in tips). Being either affluent or lucky enough to have someone serve your food doesn't allow you to overlook the basic tenets of good manners.

Acknowledge service by saying please and thank you whenever you're offered something. Neither finger clicking nor verbal rudeness is permissible: bear in mind that restaurant staff have a code of revenge for unpleasant customers.

Being either affluent or lucky enough to have someone serve your food doesn't allow you to overlook the basic tenets of good manners.

Before making additional requests (never demands), see how busy your waiter is and apologize for any extra trouble you're causing. Consideration on your part is liable to lead to better service, so everyone benefits. If you're not told, it's always a good idea to ask the member of staff looking after you what he or she is called and then use that name when making requests. If you're responsible for a large party, also tell the staff your name as this makes dealing with them much easier.

Paying the Bill

Restaurant workers are rarely paid well. When it comes to tipping, some premises include a service charge on their checks, some don't. If you're eating in one that does, ask whether the money really goes to the staff: it could instead go to boost the owner's profits. This is especially important if you're paying by credit or debit card and therefore will not be leaving any cash.

Even when you're invited to dinner by someone else, it's courteous to propose that you pay or split the cost.

The service charge is not a legal obligation. You have a choice over how much to give; this varies from one part of the world to the next, so if you're not sure, ask a local for advice. Of course you are also entitled to leave no tip. If the food and service were equally terrible, now you have an opportunity to reciprocate.

And so to settling the check (bill). Even when you're invited to dinner by someone else, it's courteous to propose that you pay or split the cost. If you're the host, you will naturally turn down this proposal. If you're a guest, once your kind offer has been declined, just accept the hospitality. But if you want to demonstrate your appreciation, propose buying a round of after-dinner drinks either in the restaurant or somewhere else. If this is also refused, there still remains an alternative: arrange to reverse roles and take your host out to dinner.

If you're having dinner with one or more friends—unless you're on a date—agree to split the cost equally. This should be so regardless of the other diners' gender: the days of a woman not paying her own way have long since passed. The check should be divided equally between all members of the group, regardless of who ate and drank what. You really do not want to end what until now has been an enjoyable evening quibbling over who of you ordered the extra side salad or drank the most wine.

The only exception should be when one member of the party has agreed to be designated driver. This person should not be required to pay for any alcohol consumed and furthermore ought to be offered a decent discount in return for saving the rest of you the price of a cab ride.

Chapter 4

The Perfectly Behaved Host

Despite the ability of some people to make it look effortless, being a good host is neither easy nor suited to everyone. No matter how hard you try, it could be that your parties prove as triumphant as a fallen soufflé. Perhaps you are trying too hard: never play host if you're going to be tense and nervous before, during, and after the event. It's essential that you feel comfortable when entertaining. Guests take their cue from the host, and your mood sets the tone for everyone else present.

Bear in mind that the people you've invited are your friends. They'll still love you even if you're not a cordon bleu cook or champion cocktail mixer. In other words, operate within your comfort zone and you stand a good chance of being a successful host. This may mean coffee and a cookie are all you ever offer— so be it. Become too ambitious and you risk running into trouble. Learn from mistakes and avoid repeating them.

Above all, enjoy yourself. Make sure there's enough time before your party begins for you to relax. Have a bath or shower and a drink. Only one drink though: you don't want to be slurring your words and clutching the door handle for support when the first guests arrive.

If, after doing your best, you still find yourself not cut out for the role of host, avoid it as much as possible. Reciprocation is not the only way to repay hospitality (see "The Perfectly Behaved Guest," below).

Some General Advice

Don't be afraid to over-invite. It is a strong possibility that at least one, if not more, of your guests will cancel at the last minute. Nobody minds a social squeeze, in fact many regard this as the sign of a successful occasion. It's certainly preferable to a handful of guests timorously gazing at one another across an expanse of empty floor.

Invite early and often. Send out a "save the date" note or email as soon as you have decided when to hold a party. Follow up with a reminder or more formal invitation later. This increases the likelihood of having everybody you want at your event.

Get the mix right. Always invite a few new acquaintances, rather than just the same group of old friends. Everybody loves to broaden their social horizons, and by asking people beyond your usual social circle you can expect to receive more invitations in return.

Ask a loyal friend or two to arrive early. If you're doing everything yourself, they'll help with last-minute preparations. They will also notice if something has been forgotten, like the main dish still waiting to be put into the oven. And when the first "real" guests turn up, they'll have somebody to talk to while you get drinks.

You might even consider inviting your neighbors: they probably won't come, but it will make them more tolerant should your party be longer and louder than anticipated.

Advise your neighbors beforehand that you are having friends over, especially if you think the event might be noisy or late or lead to lots of additional cars parked in the immediate vicinity. You might even consider inviting your neighbors: they probably won't come, but it will make them more tolerant should your party be longer and louder than anticipated.

Particularly if you're expecting a large number of guests, put away anything easily breakable: alcohol consumption makes us all clumsy. At the same time, even if nobody you've invited is a smoker, place an ashtray on every surface in the room. You are entitled to forbid smoking in your home, but this interdiction

will probably not be appreciated or obeyed: hence the ashtrays. Put out lots of drinks mats; their presence will help to minimize stains on your furniture. But recognize that before the night is over at least one glass of red wine will have been spilled somewhere in the house. If you aren't prepared to accept this possibility, you'd better cancel the party now.

Hosting a Party

Whether you're having a handful of friends over for a quick drink or 200-plus for dinner and dancing, much the same rules apply. The first is that everyone says they hate these events, but everyone gives and goes to them. They continue to take place because they're the most convenient way of entertaining people and repaying hospitality. One of the problems with parties is that they require guests to stand, often without knowing anybody else in the room and without the benefit of a thoughtful host providing introductions.

Avoid introducing one guest to a multitude of others. Pick whoever is nearest and likely to be compatible.

Accordingly, the latter are vital, particularly during the early stages of the evening: inevitably the first arrivals will be strangers to one another. Traditional good manners require you to introduce a man to a woman and a younger person to the older. Today, what matters most is that you state each person's name clearly and loudly enough for it to be heard. Ideally, first and surnames should be given, but if this seems too much just the first should do. Try to avoid introducing just one guest to a multitude of others. Just pick whoever is nearest and most likely to be compatible.

With regard to this last point, it is helpful when performing introductions if you provide each person with a nugget of information about the other, preferably something that is of mutual interest. Then you can leave the two of them to pick up the thread while you move on to do the same thing elsewhere in the room. (Note to guests: if you want to be judged as perfectly behaved in your allotted role, learn how to introduce yourself and give your name clearly. Don't stand about waiting for your already harassed host to do it for you.)

As a host, it's critical that you leave yourself free to make sure guests are mixing happily. Therefore, arrange for someone else to be responsible for serving drinks. If you can't afford professional help, rope in a nephew or niece or some other young person who'll be delighted to earn a little cash. As a rule, the young love this kind of job because it makes them feel grown-up. Just make sure the amateur staff, especially if underage, don't take advantage of the opportunity to consume as much as or more than they

serve. No spare nephews or nieces? Call on the services of a friend: smart guests know nobody's more popular at a party than the person clasping a full bottle, so this is a great way to make new friends and to avoid being cornered by the inexorable bore ("I'd love  to linger and hear more about your model tank collection, but unfortunately I see someone across the room who needs a refill!").

Do serve drinkable wine: plonk will never win you that Perfect Host rosette.

If you offer a simple choice of drinks, the job of temporary bartender ought to pose no challenges. It's primarily a question of pouring and clearing. So limit the options to white and red wine—making sure the former is well chilled—together with beer if you think that might be your guests' preference, lots of water (still and sparkling), and perhaps something like an elderflower cordial. If you're feeling flush, an uncomplicated cocktail like a Sea Breeze (one-third each of grapefruit juice, cranberry juice, and vodka; mix in a jug, add ice, and pour) can be added to the range. You don't want to spend the night rattling a cocktail shaker.

Remember that the combination of white wine and sparkling water allows you to offer a spritzer, which has the additional advantage of stretching out supplies. Make sure you are well stocked with ice, and, if necessary, buy a bag or two from your local supermarket. Do serve drinkable wine: plonk will never win you that Perfect Host rosette.

You are not obliged to provide food at a party, so only offer what's within your capabilities and your budget. You should be able to stretch to a few bowls of nuts or olives, although both of these contain a lot of salt, which will stimulate thirst, in turn leading to requests for more drinks.

Canapés demand a certain amount of effort: even if bought ready-made, they still have to be laid out on plates and handed around. Make sure that whatever eatables you supply are accompanied by an abundance of paper napkins, otherwise your furniture is likely to be covered in oily finger marks.

If you want to serve something more substantial to eat, organize a one-plate buffet. The majority of your guests will be on their feet and won't want the challenge of chewing through several courses. Everything should fit onto a single plate (or better yet, a bowl) and be eaten with one implement: a fork or a spoon. On these occasions, never serve anything that needs to be cut with a knife; it's impossible to do this while standing, clutching a glass, and carrying on a conversation. Avoid serving anything that's sloppy or has lots of sauce; the first place it'll go is onto your carpet. Again, have lots and lots of napkins to hand.

When a party is in full swing, it can be difficult to persuade guests to help themselves to food. Arrange to have your helper (the aforementioned niece/nephew or friend) hand around plates of food, each accompanied by a fork and napkin. The same help can then go around clearing up plates as soon as they are no longer wanted.

Finally, you should be prepared for a handful of loitering guests who have made no plans to go on somewhere after your party. If you don't want them to stay all night, either anticipate the dawdlers by having a casual dinner prepared (and make sure anyone staying on earns a place at the table by helping to clear up), or arrange to have another engagement and use this as your reason for ejecting lingerers.

Never serve anything that needs to be cut with a knife: it's impossible to do this while standing.

The Perfectly Behaved Host **67**

Hosting a Dinner

Particularly if you intend to do everything yourself, hosting a dinner can seem daunting. The key to success is good preparation. Make a list of what you must do and then, like Santa Claus, check it twice, at least. Leave nothing to chance, or to the last minute.

First on your list should be the names of prospective guests: as with any other party, over-invite. Not everyone you ask will be free, and elbow-to-elbow around the table is better than yawning spaces between chairs: the former makes for congeniality and lively conversation, the latter encourages awkward silences.

Next, plan your menu, taking into account any dietary restrictions among your intended guests. (Note to those same guests: as soon as you're invited, tell your host if there's something you can't eat. Don't leave it until the food is placed in front of you.)

A hazard of the recent slew of cooking programs on television is that it has made many hosts wish to display their culinary skills. If you can prepare a superlative meal in advance, one that requires you to leave your guests only for a minute or two between courses, then congratulations. If, on the other hand, you are liable to spend half the evening in the kitchen preparing a last-minute sauce or arranging slivers of vegetables in ornamental patterns on half a dozen plates, you will have failed as a host. Your guests have come to see you; don't deprive them of this pleasure by being a slave to the stove.

Plan to offer plain but delicious fare, and make sure as much of it as possible can be prepared well in advance. Think in terms of instant first and last courses, perhaps smoked salmon for one and

fresh fruit or a selection of good cheeses for the other. As for the main dish, cook only what you can produce with confidence, and always practice beforehand. Stick with tried-and-tested recipes that have never been known to let you down—your guests are not guinea pigs (and you don't want to be serving those either). Have some fallback food for those occasions—which can happen to the best of us—when something does go wrong or additional guests arrive. Alternatively, have to hand the number of a good local take-out establishment.

Plan to offer plain but delicious fare, and make sure as much of it as possible can be prepared well in advance.

Serve something to eat with the drinks before dinner; it will stave off hunger pangs, especially if someone is late or there are problems in the kitchen. On a tray, arrange an assortment of nuts, olives, perhaps slivers of Spanish ham, and some napkins, and your guests can help themselves. As with other parties, provide a choice of just a few drinks: red and white wine, beer, champagne if you're feeling flush, a cocktail (but only one kind) if you want to start proceedings with a swing, and something non-alcoholic.

Serving the same wines throughout the evening is simpler than opening lots of different ones. Make sure you have enough in the house by allowing a bottle for every two people and then adding one extra. Once at table, after pouring a first glass for your guests, feel free to put bottles out and to encourage those present to help themselves—and one another.

Whether you're entertaining two or twenty, arrange the table to look as smart as possible. Use a good cloth and napkins; nothing beats crisply ironed linen for both. Have a few flowers, a small bouquet (so guests sitting opposite each other aren't trying to communicate through a jungle of foliage), or perhaps even some ivy trailing along the length of the table. Candles, like champagne, somehow manage to make the atmosphere special and also to present you and your guests in a more kindly light, so have plenty on the table and elsewhere in the room.

Traditionally, knives (right-hand side) and forks (left) are placed in order of use, working from the outside toward the center so that those needed for the first course are furthest from the plate. Napkins sit to the left of the outermost fork and on side plates if you're putting these out, while glasses belong above the knives. If you plan to serve more than one variety of wine, glasses are also arranged outward in order of use, with the one for water closest to the center.

If one or more of your guests still hasn't arrived half an hour after the requested time, don't delay going to table. You will have allowed a certain amount of leeway in your calculations for preparing dinner, but it is better to begin serving rather than risk spoiling the food—and leaving those who arrived on time ravenous and ill-tempered.

Whenever there are more than a couple of you gathering to eat, make a table plan. Work out who would best enjoy each other's company, who might not gel, who could need help, and who will

Whether you're entertaining two or twenty, arrange the table to look as smart as possible.

get on with everyone. Separate couples: they spend enough time together without needing to sit side by side at your dinner table. Traditionally, you should sit at the head, but more likely you will want to be closest to the kitchen and in a spot where you can get up or sit down without causing too much disruption to everyone else. (Plan to do all the serving and clearing yourself, otherwise conversation around the table is liable to be interrupted. If there's a great deal of clearing to be done, ask one of those present to help and then refuse all other offers of assistance.)

Separate couples: they spend enough time together without needing to sit side by side at your dinner table.

Neither equal numbers nor gender balances really matter anymore, so don't become anxious if you have neither. Similarly, if someone drops out at the last minute, don't worry, although it is useful to have a friend who can be invited instead without taking offence. Moving your guests around between courses can be very unsettling, especially if some of them are having a good conversation. On the other hand, it can be the best means to ward off an incipient row or save someone who's being ignored by neighbors to left and right. You're best advised to wait until after the entrée (main course) and then, if you must, propose a switch, the easiest and most common being that all men move a few places in the same direction. After dinner, prepare coffee (regular and

decaffeinated) and something herbal, such as peppermint or chamomile tisane. Replace the tray of pre-dinner savory nibbles with a plate of sweet things, such as squares of chocolate, sugared almonds, or nougat. Offer postprandial drinks like brandy or whisky only if you want to—after everything that's already been served, you are not under any obligation to provide a range of liquor and nightcaps.

The risks of passive smoking are now so well-known that it's really not acceptable to smoke in the house, even if you're the nicotine addict. However, recognizing humanity's frailty, the perfect host will arrange to have a space just outdoors where nicotine addicts are permitted to congregate. Note to smokers: do remember that every time you leave the dinner table you disrupt proceedings. Please minimize your absences.

Chapter 5

The Perfectly Behaved Guest

Contrary to the widely held view, being a guest does not entitle you to do nothing but enjoy hospitality. In fact, a well-behaved guest, and the one likely to receive repeat invitations, will understand his role is as important as, and complementary to, that of the host. The expression about singing for your supper was coined for good reason, so start warbling.

Invitations

Invitations, whether verbal, written, emailed or sent by carrier pigeon, must receive a prompt reply. Either you can accept or you can't. Avoid prevarication: it causes havoc with your putative host's plans. Tempted as you may be to hold out for a better offer, resist. If you're uncertain of your availability, just say no and allow someone else to be asked.

If you're unsure whether the occasion is being held for a specific purpose, such as a birthday or anniversary, just ask: you don't want to be the only person turning up without an appropriate gift. The same is true of dress codes. If you've any uncertainty about what to wear, check beforehand with your hosts. The only thing you can't ask for is a list of your fellow guests; you must wait until the date in question to discover who they are.

Perfectly behaved guests are liable to receive lots of offers, some better than others. On no account cancel a previously accepted invitation because something more tempting has come along. Not only is this extremely inconsiderate, but also it is certain that your unprincipled behavior will be discovered, and you will lose your Perfectly Behaved Guest status.

Forgotten an invitation? It can happen, but it'll be less likely if you note all appointments in a diary and consult it regularly.

Charming though they may be, it is best to ignore open invitations of the "you must drop by when in the neighborhood" variety. Either you have been asked to come on a specific date and at a specific time or you haven't. Anything else is a pleasantry, implying a compliment to the charm of your company. Should you find yourself in the aforementioned neighborhood and be seized by a desire to drop by, at least telephone beforehand to ascertain whether a visit would be welcome, or whether the people who issued the invitation even remember you.

Forgotten an invitation? It can happen, but it'll be less likely if you note all appointments in a diary and consult it regularly.

If it does happen, apologize immediately and profusely. Then send a sincere handwritten note to make your memory lapse easier to forgive.

Learn to say no, especially to kind friends who repeatedly invite you for drinks or dinner.

On the other hand, if you arrive to find that your hosts are the ones who've forgotten and are lounging on the sofa with the television remote in hand, don't stay, no matter how much you're pressed to. If they haven't made due preparations to receive you, it'll be challenging for them to whip up instant hospitality. They will forever appreciate your thoughtfulness (and remember to invite you back often) if you insist that you have something else to do and head for home.

Learn to say no, especially to kind friends who repeatedly invite you for drinks or dinner. Suppress that momentary panic that your refusal will cause offence (make sure you decline with a decent excuse) or that you will be forever dropped from the guest list. Consider yourself as like currency: the less of you in circulation, the more you're worth on any specific occasion. Don't devalue yourself by being always available.

Finally, if you have any special dietary requirements, allergies, or particular needs, advise your hosts when accepting their hospitality. Waiting until you're served a satay sauce before informing them that you can't be in the presence of a peanut is both unwise and unhelpful.

Punctuality

Be on time. "Punctuality," said Louis XVIII, "is the politeness of kings." If it was good enough for royalty, it's good enough for you. Tardiness, on the other hand, is a sign of selfishness, indicating that you believe yourself and your lousy timekeeping to be more important than everybody else. If you're unsure whether an invitation for dinner requesting your presence at 8pm for 8.30 means the first or the second, ask your host when you accept. Having clarified the matter, it's imperative that you follow instructions. If you don't know how long the journey might take, leave yourself extra time: you can always use those spare ten minutes outside your hosts' house to catch up on emails or make a call. The alternative is you sitting in bad traffic knowing that the other guests have turned up when asked and are now collectively awaiting your arrival.

Should you be running late, have the good manners to let your hosts know as soon as possible. Everyone has a cellphone, so there is no excuse for not calling with a (brief) explanation of why you haven't yet arrived, plus a plea that your absence shouldn't delay proceedings. Note, by the way, that long-winded discussions of missed turns or a babysitter's cancellation rarely hold anyone else's interest other than your own, so make explanations and apologies sincere but short.

Gifts

The perfectly behaved guest never arrives empty-handed. No matter how small, bring something with you as an indication of gratitude for the hospitality you are about to receive. Buy a plant in a garden center, pick up a bouquet of flowers (although never, under any circumstances, from a gas station), grab a box of decent chocolates or a bottle of wine. It needn't be expensive, but it should be appropriate to your hosts and their interests and to the occasion (so no coming over with a magnum of champagne when you've only been invited for tea or the people you're visiting are teetotal). Consider having a "present drawer," namely a place where you store various items that might be useful to proffer as gifts at some future date. It's possible to pick up bits and pieces when traveling that can't be found at home and will delight the recipient. If the gathering is small, hand the gift directly to your host or hostess; if large, just leave it in the entrance hall (having included a note with your name).

Behaving Perfectly at Parties

At social occasions everyone suffers to some degree from shyness or nerves; the perfectly behaved guest learns how to deal with these social hazards. Shyness is a form of selfishness: you're so busy thinking about yourself and how you feel that nobody else is of any consequence. Don't delude yourself that as a result you look mysterious and brooding. A more likely outcome is that

The Perfectly Behaved Guest **81**

you're categorized as the guest who didn't join in the conversation, preferring to appear bored and aloof.

Shyness is a form of selfishness: you're so busy thinking about yourself and how you feel that nobody else is of any consequence.

One way to avoid this fate is through acquiring certain easily learned skills, most obviously by always having something to say for yourself. Read a newspaper, listen to the radio, watch the television news, and you will have an abundance of topics for discussion, more than enough to carry you through any encounter. Show an interest in the people to whom you are speaking: ask questions, such as where are they from, what do they do, and so forth. Their answers will provide you with leads for further questions or a more general conversation, whether about children's schooling or the weather or the state of the nation. Accept that the subject under consideration might not always be of great interest, but it helps get the conversational ball rolling.

Breaking the Ice

As a rule, we are all inclined to speak with most relish about ourselves and what matters to us. Encourage other people to do just that and you'll soon gain a reputation for being intelligent and considerate. Likewise, look out for other shy folk and see what you can do to help. Remember the occasions when you've appreciated interest from a fellow guest, and make sure that no one's left standing alone and apparently friendless.

Understand the difference between a monologue and a conversation, and stick with the latter.

Resist the seemingly attractive option of taking refuge in alcohol. It is a chimera liable to leave you with a hangover and everyone else wishing never to encounter you again. Likewise, avoid verbosity: playing Mr. Chatterbox will merely have the effect of making you seem vainglorious.

Understand the difference between a monologue and a conversation, and stick with the latter. Unlike the monologue, good conversation is essentially a team sport, in which everyone

present gets an equal chance to participate. Many men are inclined to treat social occasions as an opportunity to run through their repertoire of jokes. Under no circumstance begin a sentence with the phrase "This will amuse you," or embark on a long-winded anecdote. If you want to be a stand-up comedian, go onstage. The urge to show off in company is a powerful one, but it must be suppressed: the evening's original plan almost certainly didn't include you demonstrating your ability to remember a lengthy and complicated joke or speaking in supposedly funny voices.

Face up to "foot-in-mouth" syndrome. No matter how polite, well-mannered, or considerate you are, it's likely that sooner or later you'll commit a verbal faux pas, such as speaking ill of someone who turns out to be your host's sister or trashing the taste of someone else in the room. Should this occur, immediately find out the nature of your offence and, regardless of what you might really think or feel, apologize. Trying to make a joke about what's happened or blustering that people shouldn't be so thin-skinned will only make a bad situation worse. If you are a witness to someone else's faux pas, see what, if anything, you can do to smooth matters over quickly. Once the error has been recognized and apologies have been made (and, one hopes, accepted), help the awkwardness to pass speedily by introducing another topic of conversation.

Avoid Putting One's Foot in It

If you hold strong opinions about religion or immigration or sexual behavior or any other subject known to be divisive and possibly objectionable, keep them to yourself when socializing. There are plenty of opportunities to exchange views on such topics in a public forum, whether in person or online. But a dinner table isn't a debating chamber, so don't treat it as such. If someone else initiates a conversation of this kind, try not to become immersed in too serious a discussion if you suspect that it might turn unpleasant and move to another topic just as soon as you can.

When socializing, you have an obligation to consider the feelings of others.

Don't use bad language in company. However, don't be shocked when other people ignore this rule. Curses debase all language, particularly when employed repeatedly. They imply a limited vocabulary and want of imagination. They also risk causing offence. When socializing, you have an obligation to consider the feelings of others, no matter how different they might be from your own. Curse with gusto when alone, if you wish, but curb the habit in company. And if someone else does it, resist the temptation to tut.

Old-fashioned table manners, such as not putting your elbows on the table or talking to the person on one side of you for the first course and then whoever is on the other for the next (having taken a cue from your hostess), count for very little today, so don't worry too much if you get something wrong. It isn't of much consequence if you use an incorrect spoon; it is of great import if you rudely draw attention to someone else's social solecisms. Demonstrate flawless manners and effortless consideration by putting other people at their ease.

Find ways to assist your hosts, who will most likely be distracted trying to introduce guests, serve drinks, prepare food, or clear the table. Under those circumstances, it's possible they don't notice that a member of the party has been left with nobody to talk to. At the dinner table, check that everyone in your vicinity has whatever they need, whether it's the salt and pepper or a refill of their wineglass. See what you can do to help and thus hasten your ascent into the pantheon of perfectly behaved guests.

Retain a modicum of formality with your hosts, however. No matter how well you know them, and how often they've entertained you, the indisputable fact remains: you're a guest and you continue to have certain obligations. Remember that there is an invisible but very real boundary you are not permitted to cross, so no helping yourself to another drink without first asking permission, no taking food from the refrigerator, no changing the music on the stereo.

When in someone else's house, venture only where you're permitted to go. If you enter the kitchen, understand that you're there for a purpose: lingering at the door, large drink in hand, while your hosts are frantically putting together dinner for a dozen imminently expected guests is not helpful. Some hosts don't like anyone else seeing them at work or indeed the conditions in which they work (entrée coming out of a series of prepared packets, yesterday's plates still congealing in the sink), and they are likely to have organized a system that your presence will only disrupt. Offer to help, whether with dicing vegetables or clearing away dishes, but accept that the offer might be declined. You can be just as much use keeping the other guests entertained

Remember there is an invisible but very real boundary you are not permitted to cross, so no changing the music.

before or during the meal; recall to yourself the line of John Milton: "They also serve who only stand and wait."

Know when to leave. Your departure from any social occasion ought to be as well-timed as your arrival. If the group is small, say goodbye to everyone; if it's large, restrict yourself to whoever's in your immediate vicinity. It is better to slip away than to make a showy exit, as this can interrupt conversation elsewhere in the room. Thank your hosts before you go and insist that you don't need to be accompanied to the door; they'll probably ignore your plea, but make it anyway. At very big gatherings, when you see your hosts in the distance, just leave: you can give an explanation later when you write to send your fulsome thanks for their hospitality. Above all, regardless of how much you are pressed to stay, never ever be the last person to make an exit. The one thing you want to leave behind is a longing for more of your company. This is less likely to be the case if you're still holding forth (and holding a large drink) in the early hours of the morning. Once you see the first guest saying their farewells, follow suit.

Finally, show your gratitude, and do so every time you have enjoyed someone else's hospitality. Don't take it for granted, otherwise you could find you're not asked back. The best way to indicate your appreciation is by writing. A good thank-you letter will always endear you to hosts. You don't have to be intensely literary or witty in your correspondence (although it helps): clear evidence of gratitude is your best asset. Be specific rather than general in your remarks. Instead of simply saying that you loved the food, mention one dish in particular, or refer to a lively conversation, or another guest whose company you especially enjoyed. Length isn't necessarily important—a well-composed postcard will do the trick.

If you don't feel up to the task of composing a letter or card, make a telephone call, or send an email, or even a funny text. These are particularly permissible if similar methods were used to invite you. If your company was requested on a formal white card, an emailed thank-you isn't really satisfactory, but nor is a long letter written after a casual drinks party to which you were asked by text. What matters most is that you are prompt. Ideally write the following day and absolutely within a week of the event.

Chapter 6

Perfect Behavior on Formal Occasions

Luckily, formal social occasions don't occur all that often, but such events— weddings, significant birthdays, and other milestones—deserve to be marked with a certain solemnity and a lot of laughter. If you're the person celebrating such a moment in your life, consider sending out a printed invitation, not least because it will immediately alert your intended guests to the fact that this is not just another party.

Invitations

Invitations of this sort are expensive, but like special occasions, they are also now rare and worth the cost. However, if you can't afford to spend money on a professionally printed invitation, design one on your computer (or have a technologically savvy child do it for you) and run off as many copies as are needed on your home printer. For formal occasions, an email invitation is insufficiently substantial.

The key pieces of data on your invitation are as follows: who is hosting the event; when and where it will take place; the reason for the party; the type of occasion; how guests are to dress; and, finally, how invitees should let you know whether or not they can attend. Covering all these points leaves nothing to chance or speculation. Write the name of the person you are asking at the top of the invitation: it personalizes the request.

Make it clear what kind of party you're asking guests to attend. Yes, it's a wedding, but where will it be held? Today, couples are as likely to plight their troth in a cattle shed as in a church. Give guidance, not least to the question of appropriate dress (especially if you really are getting married in a cattle shed). Although a few people might object to being told what to wear, the majority of your guests will appreciate some help in this matter.

Note to guests: if the invitation specifies a suit but you hate wearing one, get over your grumbling and get into a suit. The person at the center of this occasion isn't you but someone else, someone who has been kind enough to ask you along. Now display a little reciprocal consideration.

As host, make sure you get the guests you want by dispatching invitations or at least a "save the date" note or email as early as possible. If you're celebrating your fiftieth birthday with a weekend in a hired villa in Tuscany, invitees will really appreciate being given plenty of notice so they can book reasonably priced flights (and thereby have more money left to spend on a gift for you). For major events, such as weddings, the invitation proper ought to be mailed to prospective guests between six weeks and two months beforehand.

Mailing invitations well in advance also indicates that you'd like to know promptly who will and won't be coming. Putting the letters RSVP ("répondez s'il vous plaît") in the bottom left-hand corner of your invitation will encourage recipients to let you know. Below this, give an address, telephone number, and/or email address to which replies can be sent. If you wish, give a deadline for responses. While this can look a little bossy, it certainly helps when finalizing matters like the catering. Alternatively, you might include another card with the invitation, a reply form that confirms whether the person invited can come. A pre-addressed envelope, one that comes with a stamp, will also help guarantee a good rate of response. Incidentally, you can also include on the invitation details of local accommodation, if some of the people coming along will need to stay overnight.

Another note to guests: your hosts have gone to all this trouble to invite you to their special occasion. Do the decent thing and reply with due haste. You are allowed to bring someone else with you only if the invitation specifies it ("John Doe and Partner"), otherwise not. The same rule applies to children: don't assume they'll be welcome if it's not stated. When replying, make it clear whether you are coming alone or with the aforementioned partner or child (giving their name, in case there are to be table plans). If you can't bear the thought of turning up on your own, don't go at all. Again, keep in mind that you are a secondary player in this event, not one of the principals, although even those with walk-on parts can make a difference to the overall success of the occasion.

Weddings and Civil Ceremonies

Barely half a century ago, couples would get hitched with just a handful of witnesses, grab a drink in a local bar or pub, and then return to work. Today there exists a dauntingly lucrative wedding industry, and apart from taking on a mortgage, getting married can be the greatest expense a couple will ever face. Without wishing to rain on your choreographed parade involving dozens of bridesmaids and pageboys, you and your loved one should try to remember that a lot of effort and money are being lavished on just one day in your lives together, a day during which you are likely to be so frazzled that photographs will provide your only recollection of the occasion. Try to keep things in perspective, and don't forget that what matters most is that everyone present—both of you and all your guests—enjoy themselves. Nothing is of as much consequence as that.

In the months, and especially the days, leading up to The Day, do your utmost to avoid rows. Inevitably there will be vexations and moments when you wish you could remain single, but don't allow these to deflect you from your purpose. Focus on the fact that regular, histrionic-free life will resume soon and that most likely today's crisis will become tomorrow's amusing dinner-party story. Let others around you behave badly or make absurd demands, but never allow yourself be accused of these offences

It helps if you and your partner work out far in advance what kind of event you want to hold and how much money you are prepared to spend. Try to match the former to the latter, but expect a certain amount of compromise to be necessary. Thereafter don't waver, no matter what the temptation. Next, draw up an action plan and a timetable on which all preparatory arrangements are shown chronologically. If your budget permits, hire a wedding planner: you have better things to do with your time than worry about what to do at the open-air ceremony in the event of a downpour or how to have your joint initials written in the sky with fireworks.

As a rule, bachelor (stag) parties aren't known for everyone being on best behavior: the well-mannered bachelor party would probably be regarded as a catastrophic failure. But that doesn't mean the only alternative is behaving very badly. Spare a thought for other people's feelings. If your group stays in the restaurant until four o'clock in the morning, so, too, do some of the staff, waiting to clear up after you. And if the same group then spontaneously bursts into song or argument on the street outside, the people who'll remember your bachelor party best are local residents kept awake by the racket.

On the day itself, if you're the groom, expect to be nervous. Don't worry if you fumble your lines or drop the ring or trip on your way down the aisle: it will all be found endearing by your guests. Do remember to thank all those responsible for helping to make the occasion a success and your parents-in-law for having produced someone as wonderful as your other half.

The Best Man

The duties of best man are actually more onerous. You must perform two tasks with equal aplomb, the first being standing beside the groom before the ceremony begins and to produce the wedding ring(s) at the appropriate moment. To make sure nothing goes wrong, put the ring(s) into your jacket pocket the night before the wedding, just before you and the groom go for a drink. That way, it'll be in the right place when required. Second, you are required to make a speech at the post-ceremony reception. As with so much else in life, good preparation is invaluable. Write down what you are going to say and then memorize the key points. Practice delivering your speech. If necessary, bring a few notes, but don't read them out, no matter how apprehensive you feel: your delivery will suffer. It helps if you're funny; it doesn't if you're smutty. Keep your remarks clean and keep them brief: that way you will gain lots of compliments for your ability as a public speaker.

Groomsmen (ushers) are expected to direct guests to their seats before the wedding ceremony and escort one of the countless bridesmaids out of the church afterward. Plus, they stand in the

back row of group photographs looking redundant. Later, they huddle together at the bar, passing lascivious remarks about women before one of them is discovered in the parking lot with a bridesmaid. Just make sure it isn't you (someone will inevitably record the moment and post it on YouTube).

Weddings can be romantic occasions. Nevertheless, don't get so carried away that you propose to someone else, particularly if you're already married. Don't become so drunk that you heckle the best man through his speech, grope the bride's mother, fight with one of the other guests, throw up on the dance floor, or pass out in the shrubbery. You are permitted to request one song from the DJ: he would really appreciate it if you could say please and thank you, and not ask for something he's already played half a dozen times.

Gifts

Gifts are customarily given to a newly married couple. If you are getting married, it's sensible to tell guests what you'd like to receive, otherwise you're going to end up with a lot of arcane kitchen utensils. For this reason, a wedding list, featuring a range of items you'd actually like to receive and currently stocked by one or more stores, is recommended. When sending guests their invitations, include a note giving details of the store(s). Take different budgets into account: not all your guests are able to afford to buy themselves, let alone you, a new microwave. Include a few inexpensive items, such as sets of table mats or napkins, on the list. They probably won't be ordered (no one wants to look tightfisted), but their presence will show consideration. Keep a note of who's given you what and mention the gift when writing to say thanks (a task to be accomplished within days of returning from your honeymoon). If you're both beyond first youth and already well stocked with casserole dishes and sets of sherry glasses, propose that guests make a donation to a charity of your choice instead.

Guests: you might dislike wedding lists, but they ensure the married couple get what they want. Offer a gift reflecting their taste, not your own, no matter how superior you think the latter. If no wedding list is forthcoming, ask the couple what they'd like or need. They'll then be able to let you know that they already own more than enough sherry glasses. Don't bring your wedding present to the wedding, or someone else will have to make sure it doesn't go home with one of the waiters. Send it either before or after the occasion. Guests invited to a wedding but unable to attend should nevertheless send a gift. Its purpose is to indicate that you wish the couple well in their future together.

A Few Points about Funerals

If you know the deceased or the bereaved well enough, telephone after the death and before the funeral to ask if you can help in any way. Death, especially when it's sudden or unexpected, can leave even the most capable of us incapacitated. Under these circumstances, while your services probably won't be needed, your thoughtfulness will be appreciated. And sometimes being a good listener is the best service you can provide. Ask the bereaved if he or she would like company or conversation, but don't force the issue: some people like to be left alone with their grief.

Attend the funeral service if you can. Be punctual. At a wedding you ought to be in your place before the bride, at a funeral before the coffin. If you're late to arrive, stand at the back. Be discreet. Although funerals can often be large social gatherings, they're not parties and they shouldn't be treated as such. Nor are they opportunities for networking or conducting business. Show some respect, please.

Offer your condolences to the bereaved briefly, because a lot of other people will want to do the same. A funeral line isn't the place for long-winded reminiscences; if you've more to say about the deceased, write a letter. Go to the home of the bereaved only if you're invited—don't presume that you'll be welcome.

After the funeral, send a card or letter to the bereaved. Write at the top "No Reply Necessary." A widow(er), son, or daughter can receive hundreds of such letters, and replying to them all is an exhausting business, especially at such a difficult time. If you are unsure what to write, it is enough to offer your condolences.

Grief takes a long time to pass. Even though the funeral was held a fortnight ago, your responsibilities aren't necessarily over. Keep a watching brief on someone who has been bereaved. Your support, although not needed at the time of death and burial, could make all the difference six months later when other friends have dropped away.

Chapter 7

Perfect Romantic Behavior

———◆———

Love is, of course, a many-splendored
thing, but it is also well behaved. Want
the object of your affection to feel the
same way about you? A good start is by
demonstrating you're capable of thinking
about someone other than yourself and
showing due solicitousness. This applies
whether you're on a first date or married
for thirty-plus years: some rules
never change.

There are many advantages to being single. You can watch whatever you want whenever you want on television without fighting over the remote control. The same goes for what you eat and drink, how you dress, and how late you come home after a night out. You also don't have to share a bathroom (with the inevitable repeated requests to put the seat down on the lavatory and the cap back on the toothpaste); you don't have to explain where you've been nor with whom; and you don't have to listen to complaints that you never want to talk in the morning.

Nevertheless, there is likely to come a time, possibly several times, when despite the allure of a single life you find yourself helplessly and romantically involved with someone else. The involvement might not last forever, but while it continues, you ought to behave well, if only so that should the relationship come to an end there can be no recriminations over your appalling conduct. Understand that this involves a certain level of effort and preparednesss to compromise, but all being well the trade-off will prove worthwhile.

You won't find love while sitting on the sofa at home. If you want to meet someone special, get out and mingle. There's no perfect place to find your partner, but the odds improve if you're somewhere that reflects your shared interests: that is why advice columnists regularly propose that the best way to meet new people is by joining clubs and social groups or going to night school. It's also why so many of us meet our future partners courtesy of a mutual friend.

If friends, relations, and the local golf club all fail to deliver a prospective partner, take charge of the situation and look at other options, such as dating agencies, personal advertisements, and the

You won't find love while sitting on the sofa at home. If you want to meet someone special, get out and mingle.

Internet. Contrary to the out-dated beliefs of some, these aren't suitable only for serial killers or the congenitally hopeless, but rather people who are short of time or who would prefer simply to cut to the chase.

If you're meeting someone through one of these means, note the following advice. Be honest beforehand. Don't knock off ten years, add six inches (to any part of your anatomy), or claim a PhD when you abandoned formal education at age sixteen.

Be honest, too, about what you're looking for, whether it's a long-term relationship or an hour-long encounter. Meet in a public place, and let a close friend know what you're doing, or leave a note at home—just in case the other person really is an aspiring serial killer …

Even if you take a dislike to the other person on sight, have the courtesy to remain for one cup of coffee or stiff drink.

Having agreed to meet, keep the appointment and turn up on time. Even if you take a dislike to the other person on sight, have the courtesy to remain for one cup of coffee or stiff drink. Then you can make your excuses and leave. Again, be honest and say if you think there will be no second meeting. Don't be upset if the other person calls a halt to the meeting soon after it has begun: both of you have to feel there's the possibility you have a future together. Just because you feel the stirrings of attraction, it isn't automatically reciprocal.

Going on a Date

If you want to ask someone out on a date, then do so. Make your intentions clear (i.e. say that it isn't just a social drink) and accordingly be prepared for refusal. If, on the other hand, your offer is accepted, follow it up by asking where and when would best suit, to show that you're a considerate man who takes other people's concerns into account.

First dates are like actors' auditions, where you're hoping to land the role without being completely sure it's right for you. At the back of both your minds will be lurking the same question: will there be a second meeting? Don't overburden the occasion with too many expectations. The purpose of a first date is to demonstrate whether the two of you discover a certain level of compatibility. Never assume that a date will yield immediate dividends: you bought dinner, not the other person's body for the night. Appreciation of your generosity can be expressed in words as well as actions, and even though you'd prefer the latter, the former might be all that's offered. If you move in for a kiss and are met by a turned cheek, so be it.

Make a good impression by taking a little trouble over your appearance. You don't need to have a total makeover, but try showering beforehand and putting on a clean shirt.

Keep the conversation moving. Nervousness is inclined to make some of us garrulous and to silence others. Avoid falling into either category. Be enthusiastic but not too eager, and talkative but not to the point where your date never gets a chance to speak. Ask the other person about her/himself, otherwise you'll never discover how much, or little, you have in common. Don't discuss only yourself and your many achievements across a diverse range of fields. This is a common male failing when trying to impress: it doesn't. Don't speak endlessly about your exes, especially if you haven't a kind word to say about any of them. After a first date, no matter how keen you are, don't get in touch too soon. Making contact within twenty-four hours will have you looking a little needy, but leaving it more than three days suggests indifference.

Don't discuss only yourself and your many achievements across a diverse range of fields— a common male failing when trying to impress.

Getting Personal

If things go well on the first date—the two of you laugh at the same things, engage in a lot of eye contact, find your hands brushing against each other, and so forth—at some point you're likely to move from a public to a private environment.

Make a good impression in the bedroom, and not just through your athletic prowess. The room itself should be well-aired and tidy, as should the bed: a fetid atmosphere is no inducement to passion. On the night in question, your sheets ought to be clean even if your intentions aren't. Think soft lighting (most people are naturally inclined to be self-conscious when undressing in front of someone else for the first time), adequate warmth (it's hard to have hot sex in a cold climate), and sufficient comfort (the sort provided by a decent mattress).

Your sheets ought to be clean even if your intentions aren't.

Think also adequate protection. Carrying a condom does not imply that you're a promiscuous stud; it indicates that you quite correctly have your own—and your potential partner's—well-being in mind. Small and easily dropped into a pocket, condoms remain a reliable (although not infallible) method of avoiding both unwanted pregnancy and the transmission of sexually transmitted diseases. On the subject of which, if you have an STD of any sort, you must inform the other person before anything more than conversation occurs between the two of you.

Despite what you see in the cinema, the first sexual encounter between two (or more) people isn't always characterized by an unbridled frenzy of passion and a lot of noisy exclamations. Sometimes it can be rather mediocre. However, practice frequently makes, if not perfect, then certainly better, so don't be too disappointed if on that initial occasion the earth stays firmly in place. Just like the first date between the two of you, the whole occasion can have the character of an audition. Getting to know each other's bodies takes time, patience, and courtesy, as well as a certain amount of good humor and honesty (the basis of all successful relationships). Allow for the possibility that your partner may not want to do the same thing as you, nor so often, nor indeed in front of a group of strangers in a public parking lot. Each of you must make allowances for the other: that way you can reach compatibility.

If you're not in your own home, always ask if you may stay the night. If, on the other hand, you want to go back to your own home, say and do so. Likewise, if it's your place and you want to sleep alone, make this clear (in these circumstances, offer a bed

elsewhere in the house should one be available: finding a taxi at four in the morning is never easy). If you're spending the night together, try not to take up most of the bed, snore, or hog the covers.

Serial one-nighters learn to travel with a disposable toothbrush and a comb.

The following morning, depending on whether you are taking the role of host or guest, offer or ask for the use of a bathroom and preferably a few necessities, such as a clean towel. It's always a good idea to carry some gum or other breath freshener. Serial one-nighters learn to travel with a disposable toothbrush and a comb.

Regardless of how good or bad the previous night's experience (and how much or little you can remember of what took place), be courteous and appreciative—and try to recall the other person's name. On the other hand, don't make promises you have no intention of keeping. If you are unlikely to telephone, avoid saying you will.

If it turns out to be a one-night stand and not the start of a lifelong relationship, that's no reason to shed your manners as fast as you did your clothes. Never ignore someone with whom you had any kind of intimate relationship, even if only a brief encounter. Despite your primary feeling being embarrassment or shock or (occasionally) disgust, acknowledge that you've met before and then, unless a second night together seems possible, move on.

PDAs (Public Displays of Affection/Anger) offer the rest of us TMI (Too Much Information) and ought to be curbed. No matter how strong your feelings, keep them in check when mixing with other people. Hand-holding or a little gentle chiding is permissible; anything stronger is not.

Your Romantic Life and your Family and Friends

Very often, when seeing someone new, we want to introduce them to the rest of our world. Take your time, however. If the two of you have a future together, there will be plenty of opportunities in the years ahead for tea with Great-Aunt Mabel. Rushing the procedure can leave you with a lot of explanations to make should the relationship founder not long after it has begun. In any case, a new partner will probably want to spend time primarily with you, not with your extended family, so for the moment minimize encounters of this sort.

Don't expect family and friends to feel quite as passionately about your girl/boyfriend as you do. If they did, they'd be dating her/him instead. Resist asking for their opinion of your new love: they'll let you know their thoughts if they want to do so. And make sure you're introduced to your partner's social world, too. There's something suspect about anyone who doesn't seem to have any friends.

Your personal life is a source of abiding interest to you, but not necessarily to everyone else. Don't test the patience of family and friends by talking endlessly about the current state of your love life. No matter how new the relationship and how much you're in love, stay in touch with your established circle. These are

When dating someone:

- In public, avoid looking at other women (or men, depending on your preferences).

- Resist the temptation to flirt with anyone else, or to pass extravagant compliments. Instead, remember to compliment your partner on her/his appearance. You did it when the two of you first met, so why stop now?

- Likewise, no matter how long you've been together, regularly give your partner small, thoughtful gifts.

- Try to remember anniversaries (the first time you met, the date of your wedding/civil partnership, your spouse/partner's birthday).

- Be appreciative and show gratitude for acts of kindness, no matter how small they are or how often they've been performed. Say please and thank you. Never take anything or anyone for granted.

- Don't become complacent, about yourself, about your boy/girlfriend, about your relationship.

the people to whom you'll turn when the romance hits a difficult patch, as it inevitably will, and they're much less likely to be available if you haven't spoken to them for months because of your romantic entanglements. Make time for friends now and they'll make time for you later.

Equally, if a friend embarks on a new relationship, accept that he's going to be around less, at least for the time being. Find someone else to play tennis with on Saturday morning or meet for a drink midweek. When you're eventually introduced, be pleasant to his new partner, but not too pleasant too fast. If the relationship falters, your friend will most likely expect support from you, and this will be harder to give should you have become equally close to the partner.

If you don't like the latest object of your friend's affection, keep your opinion to yourself, unless you know she has had three husbands, all of whom died in suspicious circumstances. Do so even should the relationship come to an end: the two of them could still get back together, and then your criticisms will return to haunt you.

All's Well that Ends Well

A successful relationship is based on mutual honesty, so if it's not working for you, say so. There's no point in pretending things are good when they're not.

Tell your partner how you feel as frankly but considerately as possible. A respectful explanation should help the soon-to-be ex come to terms with the change. It also forces you to articulate precisely what, in your opinion, has altered between the pair of you, which is no bad thing either.

Always end a relationship in person, not by telephone, text, email, or letter—or, worst of all, by silence and a refusal to respond to all efforts to contact you. Telling someone it's over

won't be easy; whether you're the one leaving or the one being left, brace yourself for a tsunami of confusion, anger, and hurt. Retaining control of your emotions will not be easy, and there are bound to be difficult moments. Try not to let these damage your long-term attitude toward a former partner.

> *Telling someone it's over won't be easy;*
> *whether you're the one leaving or the one being*
> *left, brace yourself for a tsunami of*
> *confusion, anger, and hurt.*

If the other side finds it hard to accept that circumstances have changed and proposes counseling, go along with the suggestion even if you're convinced it would be a waste of time and money. After all, you've probably been wrong before and you could be wrong again. Whatever the outcome, it'll help both of you acknowledge that something fundamental has gone wrong.

If you're leaving for someone else, say so from the start. You may think dissimulation is the kindest approach, but your ex won't agree: there's nothing worse than lies being exposed at a later date.

If you're the one being left, accept reality with as much grace as you can muster. Try not to complain too much about what has happened; even best friends grow tired of listening to tales of a former partner's dreadful behavior. As with all human experiences, you're not the first person to have gone through this. It's normal, it happens to all of us, and life goes on—and so will you. Recrimination is unlikely to change matters and most likely won't make you feel any better either, so avoid it. In fact, the only outcome will be to make the person leaving you even more convinced that they made the right decision.

It is inadvisable, especially if the atmosphere between you is thick with bitterness and acrimony, to express a wish that you might remain friends. Friendship is rarely found in the immediate aftermath of a breakup, but it can follow once time has had an opportunity to do its healing work. Should you meet your ex, overcome the urge to flee—or to fight—and instead take the proverbial deep breath, raise a smile, and say something courteous in greeting. No bickering, please. Keep the exchange short and sweet, then make your excuses and exit, congratulating yourself on your maturity. If you meet your ex and one or other of you is with someone new, appreciate that this is tricky for all parties, so, again, try not to use the opportunity for scoring points. You may not have retained your partner, but you can keep your dignity.

Chapter 8

Perfectly Behaved Communication

As a result of technological advances, the
means by which we communicate with
one another is constantly in flux. But the
manner in which we do so should remain
the same. Even when sending a text or
firing off an email, take trouble over your
language and make sure you display the
same civility you would in conversation.
And never underestimate the impact
of a hand-written letter.

Letters

Despite the diverse alternatives now available, letters remain a special way of keeping in touch. In fact, rarity has increased their value: texts and emails are easy to dash off, whereas letters demand greater effort to compose and are accordingly the more appreciated. Most of the mail we receive today is either bills or junk, so a letter really stands out as something special.

Never worry that you lack sufficient letter-writing skills, although if your handwriting is illegible, type out the text (with a line explaining the necessity). There are times when nothing but a letter will suffice, such as an expression of love or when someone you know has been bereaved. If you're afraid that you don't know the right way to express yourself, begin the letter by saying so: there's no shame in admitting that you have trouble coming up with the right words.

There are times when nothing but a letter will suffice, such as an expression of love or when someone you know has been bereaved.

Cards don't take as long to write, but they can be appreciated just as much. When traveling, pick up some attractive ones, perhaps in a museum or gallery, and keep them for when you need them. When writing postcards on vacation, keep your handwriting legible (best to get this job done before that second glass of wine at lunch). Make sure the recipient will have an idea who you are. We've all received cards from overseas bearing an undecipherable signature.

Those concerned about spelling and grammar should invest in a pocket dictionary, along with a simple guide to writing, such as *Fowler's Modern English Usage*. Or look up what you need online. Avoiding errors of spelling, grammar, and punctuation is particularly important in business correspondence: a misplaced apostrophe indicates lack of professionalism.

Handwritten business letters were last seen in the nineteenth century. So, no matter how beautiful your calligraphy, correspondence relating to your professional life ought to be typed and printed on the best paper you (or your company) can afford. If you work for yourself, your own stationery looks most professional and easily can be produced at home thanks to modern portable printers. Just as the letter needs to look polished, so should its tone and content be. Even when writing to someone you know well, if the context is business, it's best to

adopt a slightly impersonal style. If you wish to include a personal message in the letter, write it at the bottom of the page or on a separate note enclosed in the same envelope.

Emails

You're likely to use email in your professional and personal life alike, but once more it's recommended that you distinguish between the two. In work, the tone of your emails ought to be less jocular and more formal than would otherwise be the case. Because the medium is instant, it encourages casualness. Beware of allowing this to happen to your business emails: the recipient might get the impression that you're not serious about your work and react to you accordingly. All Internet service providers offer free email addresses. Get one for your personal use and, if you have not been supplied an address by your company, one for professional use. Keeping them separate will make it much easier to compartmentalize your business email correspondence.

Just because you are using email, do not assume that the usual rules of spelling and grammar have become irrelevant. They haven't, so carefully check what you've written before sending it. As soon as you press the "Send" button, an email is out of your hands and out of your control, so be careful: anything you write might travel far beyond the intended recipient.

Reply to all emails promptly, so that they don't build up and become a terrifying burden. Also, a speedy response is polite and will win you admiration. Particularly in the realm of business, if you expect to be incommunicado for any longer than a day or two, leave a message explaining your temporary absence. It will automatically be sent to anyone who emails and will explain why there's no response from you.

Just because you are using email, do not assume that the usual rules of spelling and grammar have become irrelevant.

Everyone who has an email address is entitled to keep it private. Don't send a group email that carries the addresses of all your other correspondents. It is also wise to be prudent when pressing "Reply"—a miscued click on the "Reply All" button has resulted in the undoing of many regretful men.

Chain emails, the kind that promise a lottery win or romantic fulfillment if you forward the message to another ten people, are infantile and annoying. A dire warning is usually attached, detailing what will happen to the unfortunate person who doesn't follow instructions. Be brave, delete the message, and discover that it makes no difference.

Speed is one of the greatest advantages of email, but it's also one of its greatest hazards. If you write an email when angry, upset, or drunk, let it sit overnight. Even if your mood hasn't changed by the following morning, your ability to write a coherent sentence will certainly have done so.

Speed is one of the greatest advantages of email, but it's also one of its greatest hazards.

Telephones: Fixed and Mobile

At the start of a call, if there's any possibility the person you have called won't recognize your voice, give your name. It's very irritating to have an apparent stranger say "Hi, how are you?" The only response is "Hi, who are you?" Even though many phones now have caller ID, don't take it for granted that everyone knows who you are. Remember, they can't see you.

Don't forget to focus just because you're not in front of the person on the other end of the line. Turn off the television, put down the magazine, quit surfing the Internet. If you can't stop whatever it is you're doing at that moment, explain and ask if you can call back later. Then do so. If you're the caller, it's considerate to begin by asking if this is a convenient time to talk. Should the answer be negative, offer to call again and find out when would be a more suitable time.

Other than being portable, a cellphone doesn't differ from an ordinary phone. Therefore, unless the person on the other end of the line is profoundly deaf, there's no need for you to speak VERY LOUDLY.

In public places, put your cellphone on silent or vibrate. Please don't let it ring on and on and on without answering the call. Personalized ringtones are, by their nature, personal. Your taste is yours and very possibly yours alone. Keep it to yourself.

> *Treat talking on the telephone just like any other conversation: that means not making a call when you're in the lavatory.*

Apologize to other people if you have to take a call when in company, then leave the room. Return when you have finished the call.

If you possess a hands-free device and walk about in public apparently talking to yourself, you should expect everyone to cross the street as you approach.

Treat talking on the telephone just like any other conversation: that means not making a call when you're in the lavatory.

On your voicemail, give your name or some other indication that the caller has got the right number. Reply to a message promptly, otherwise there will be an understandable assumption that you didn't receive it. Check your home answering machine regularly. Even when you're away from home, it's possible to pick up messages. If you don't, your mailbox will become full and later callers might not be able to leave you a message at all.

When leaving a message, keep it short. Speak clearly and leave your name ("It's me" doesn't count), as well as the date and time of your call and your telephone number. Speak the number slowly and then repeat it, as numbers given in a mumbled or fast voice are often written down incorrectly. Ask to be called back. Then hang up.

Abbreviations in texts are permissible for teenagers, but after that it looks a bit sad, the equivalent of someone middle-aged trying to be hip by saying things like "chill out." As with skateboarding and illicit smoking behind the bicycle shed, the language of text abbreviation belongs to the young. Bear in mind, too, that not everybody will be as fluent in text-speak as u r. Some people will just assume that you can't spell very well and judge you accordingly. Keep text exchanges short—they're no substitute for a proper conversation. Don't text when you're in company: it suggests the people you're with are of lesser importance. And never give a private little smile while reading text responses.

"Selfie" was deemed by the Oxford Dictionaries to be the word of 2013. Now that year is behind us, think carefully before sending pictures on your phone, particularly of yourself. Although some forms of technology apparently allow for their rapid destruction, rest assured that someone, somewhere, will retain a copy; even now aliens on another planet might be sniggering over the size and shape of your genitalia.

Think carefully before sending pictures on your phone, particularly of yourself.

Sending someone a photograph of a beautiful sunset or posting it on a social network is fine. Sending or posting a photograph of somebody else to a third party starts raising questions about invasion of privacy. If you're sharing pictures of anyone else but yourself, first ask permission: your buddy might have told his boss he was off sick or his wife that he was away on a training day. Understand that once a picture or video is in the public domain, it doesn't go away. Ever. What's funny when you're twenty and single and yet to look for employment may be hard to explain when you're forty, married, and looking to move to a better job.

Index